Modern Industrial World

Britain

David Flint

Wayland

MODERN INDUSTRIAL WORLD

Australia	**Portugal**
Britain	**Russia**
Canada	**South Africa**
France	**Spain**
Germany	**Sweden**
Japan	**The USA**

Cover: New office developments in London's Docklands, a once run-down area that is now seeing new business and industrial growth.

Title page: Charing Cross train station in London serves London's West End and has an average of 140,000 passengers passing through it every day.

Contents page: Steam from the cooling towers of a coal-fired power station in Yorkshire. When the steam mixes with the gases from the burning coal, it adds to the problem of acid rain pollution in Britain.

Book editor: Polly Goodman
Series editor: Paul Mason
Designer: Mark Whitchurch
All map artwork by Hard Lines Cartographers.
All graph artwork by Mark Whitchurch.

First published in 1996 by
Wayland Publishers Ltd
61 Western Road, Hove
East Sussex, BN3 1JD, England

British Library Cataloguing in Publication Data
Flint, David.
   Britain. – (Modern industrial world)
   1. Britain – Juvenile literature
   I. Title
   941'.085

ISBN 0 7502 1872 X

Typeset by Mark Whitchurch, England
Printed and bound in Italy by G. Canale & C.S.p.A., Turin

Contents

Introduction

Britain is made up of three countries, England, Scotland and Wales, on an island off the coast of north-west Europe, 48 km from France. Britain is part of the United Kingdom of Britain and Northern Ireland. Since 1994, Britain has been physically linked to the rest of Europe by the Channel Tunnel, 50 km under the English Channel.

Britain has a long history as a great economic, political and military power. However in recent years, Britain's economy has suffered a series of setbacks, with the decline of traditional industries such as coal-mining, steel and car manufacturing and shipbuilding. In addition to industrial decline, Britain has lost its empire throughout the twentieth century as countries in Africa and Asia have gained their independence. Now Britain is seeking to revive its economy by establishing new industries and regaining its political importance. The British economy is still the sixth-largest in the world and Britain is still a major international force with a seat on the United Nations Security Council.

Opposite The city of Edinburgh, Scotland's capital, is dominated by its castle, to the right of the photograph.

Below Nelson's Column and the fountain of Trafalgar Square, in London's West End, is a popular tourist spot and meeting place.

Britain is a member of the European Union (EU), a group of fifteen countries made up of itself, France, Germany, Italy, Denmark, Ireland, Sweden, Finland, Austria, Spain, Portugal, Greece, the Netherlands, Belgium and Luxemburg. The European Union began in 1959 as a group of six countries (France, Germany, Italy, Netherlands, Belgium and Luxemburg).

4

The main aim of the EU was to abolish customs duties on goods traded between member states in order to stimulate the growth of trade and industry. The success of these original six countries encouraged other countries to join later. In 1973 Britain, Ireland and Denmark joined. In 1981 Greece became a member, in 1986 Spain and Portugal joined, and in 1995 Sweden, Finland and Austria also joined.

Shetland Isles

LAND HEIGHT

Land under 200 m
200–500 m
500–1,000 m

Motorways
Major roads
Railways

N

0   200 km
0   125 miles

Orkney

ATLANTIC OCEAN

Outer Hebrides

Inner Hebrides

Spey

SCOTLAND

Aberdeen

Ben Nevis
1,343 m

Dundee

NORTH
SEA

Forth

Firth of Forth

Glasgow

Edinburgh

Tweed

Firth of
Clyde

NORTHERN
IRELAND

Carlisle

Tyne

Solway Firth

Tees

Ouse

Isle of Man

IRISH SEA

Bradford

Leeds

Humber

REPUBLIC OF
IRELAND

Liverpool

Manchester

Sheffield

The Wash

Snowdon
1,085 m

Dee

Derby

Nottingham

Norwich

Leicester

Birmingham

Coventry

Cambridge

Severn

E N G L A N D

WALES

Oxford

LONDON

Swansea

Cardiff

Bristol

Thames

Bristol Channel

Channel
Tunnel

Exe

Southampton

Brighton

FRANCE

Exeter

Isle of Wight

Plymouth

ENGLISH CHANNEL

Isles of Scilly

The jagged teeth of the Cuillin Hills on the Isle of Skye show a landscape shattered by frost and ice. With thin soils, steep slopes and cold winters, farming here is almost impossible. The island's main income is from tourism, fishing and forestry.

Britain has many different landscapes, from high mountains to rolling hills and valleys. The highest areas are found in the north and west of the country, where places like Wales, the Lake District and north-west Scotland have high mountains and steep slopes carved out of solid rock. The landscape of these upland areas was shaped millions of years ago during the Ice Ages, when moving glaciers of ice created deep valleys, steep mountain slopes and long lakes. The southern and eastern parts of Britain are made up of younger, softer rocks which have weathered to become fertile farmland.

COASTS

Britain is completely surrounded by sea. At times in the country's history, the sea has been a barrier, isolating it from the rest of Europe. At other times, it has provided a way of gaining land and wealth in other countries through travel. No part of Britain is far from the sea, which is an important resource for fishing, tourism and ports. The sea-level around Britain is rising as the ice locked up in the North and South Poles melts. Since 1900 the sea-level has risen by 1 m, and the rise continues. As the sea-level rises, river valleys slowly fill with water to form wide estuaries. In Cornwall and Devon these are called rias; in Scotland, deep, U-shaped valleys called sea lochs have been filled.

RIVERS

Rivers are an important part of the British landscape. They form rapids, waterfalls and meanders as they flow from the mountains to the sea. Britain's rivers provide drinking water for towns, and irrigate farmers' crops. However, living near a river does bring problems, such as flooding. In spring, when heavy rain combines with melting snow, rivers like the Severn and the Ouse burst their banks and flood homes, factories and farmland.

BRITAIN AT A GLANCE	
Population (1992):	
England	46.2 million
Scotland	4.9 million
Wales	2.8 million
Total	53.9 million
Population density:	235 people per km^2
Life expectancy (women):	76 years
(men):	71 years
Area:	
England	130,439 km^2
Scotland	78,772 km^2
Wales	20,768 km^2
Total	229,979 km^2
Capital:	London
Longest river:	Thames, 450 km
Highest mountain:	Ben Nevis, 1,343 m
Main religion:	Christianity
Currency:	Pound sterling
Main products:	Automobiles, machinery, chemicals

Fields flooded when the banks of the River Avon burst after heavy rain. In general, large floods are not common in Britain, although some regions suffer more often than others.

CLIMATE

Britain has cool summers and mild winters, with rainfall all year round. The climate is variable, meaning that the weather changes from day to day, which makes forecasting difficult. The climate is also temperate, which means that in general the country does not have long periods when it is very hot, very cold or very wet.

Western parts of Britain receive more rain and snow during the year than the south and east. This is because south-westerly winds carry water from the Atlantic Ocean to the west, which falls as rain when it meets the mountains on land. There is a surplus of water in this area and a shortage in the south and east. As a result, reservoirs have been built in areas such as the Lake District to store water, which is then sent by pipeline to the towns of the south-east.

Britain's south coast beaches, like Kynance Cove in Cornwall, are attracting more and more visitors, particularly in good summer weather. Some of the most beautiful coastal areas have been bought by the National Trust, a conservation group that protects areas of natural beauty from being spoiled by tourism.

RISING TEMPERATURES

Britain's climate is getting warmer. Average temperatures have risen by 0.5 °C since 1850. This is enough to start the polar ice caps melting. If the ice caps continue to melt, large areas of southern and eastern England will be permanently flooded.

On average, in January, eastern Britain is colder and has less rain than the west. In July, the south is warmer than the north.

SUMMER AND WINTER TEMPERATURES

In July, the south of Britain is warmer than the north, so many tourists prefer to visit south-coast resorts with long hours of sunshine. In the winter, western areas are warmer than the east. This is because the Gulf Stream, a current of warm water, flows from the Caribbean across the Atlantic Ocean to affect western Britain. The Gulf Stream keeps ports free from ice and only allows snow to settle briefly.

JANUARY TEMPERATURES

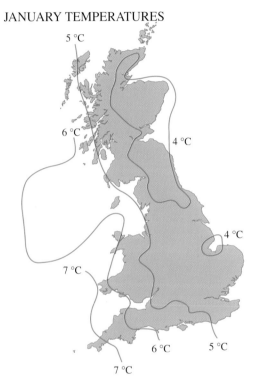

JULY TEMPERATURES

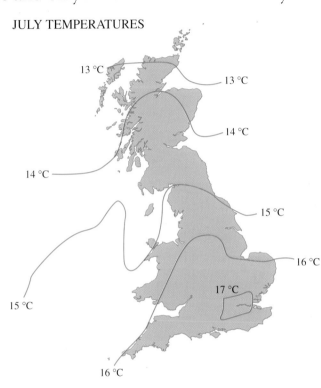

DAILY HOURS OF SUNSHINE

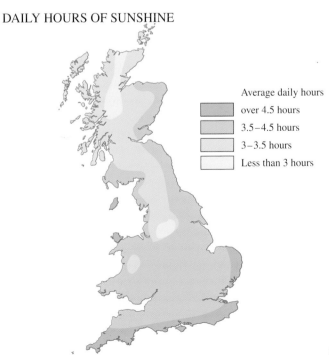

Average daily hours

- over 4.5 hours
- 3.5–4.5 hours
- 3–3.5 hours
- Less than 3 hours

AVERAGE ANNUAL RAINFALL

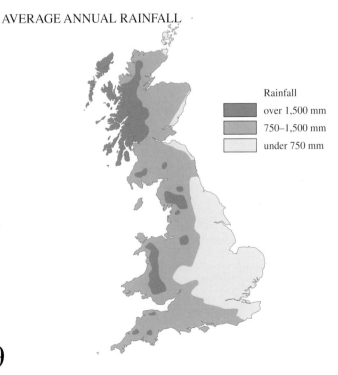

Rainfall

- over 1,500 mm
- 750–1,500 mm
- under 750 mm

WEATHER HAZARDS

From time to time Britain is affected by drought, such as those in 1976, 1984 and 1995. Water levels in reservoirs and rivers fall, and the water supply to homes, offices, farms and factories is often affected.

Fog tends to form in the autumn and winter, causing aircraft to be grounded or diverted and airports to close. Fog can also cause serious car accidents in motorway crashes. Another weather hazard is frost, which occurs from December until late spring. Frost can kill the blossom on fruit trees in spring and can combine with ice to make roads slippery.

Snow and ice can cause serious problems in winter in the northern regions of Britain. Snow can cut off roads, railway lines and power, stranding drivers and isolating homes in the coldest months of the year. Many areas of Britain are subjected to very high winds. These can disrupt transport and power supplies when fallen trees block roads and bring down power lines. High winds can also create huge waves which can flood large areas close to the sea.

The River Westend, near Sheffied, after a hot summer had lowered its water level. Since this river feeds a reservoir that supplies water to the local population, a hosepipe ban was imposed until it rained again.

Pollution of the North Sea

The North Sea has become the 'dustbin' of Europe, as the eight industrial nations around its shores use it to dispose their waste. It is a shallow sea with a current that flows anticlockwise. This current collects pollution from the rivers emptying into the sea and sweeps it along the coast. The Rhine, the Meuse and the Elbe rivers, from Germany and the Netherlands, produce most of the pollution, but British rivers such as the Thames, Tees, Tyne and Forth add to the problem.

Different types of pollution are carried by the rivers – untreated sewage from towns and cities; industrial waste, including poisonous heavy metals like mercury and arsenic; and toxic, agricultural chemicals which have been washed from the land into the rivers. The North Sea is also polluted by oil from offshore oil wells, production platforms and oil tankers based in its waters.

The effects of the pollution have been drastic. Tourism has declined in some resorts because of polluted waters and dirty beaches. Many fish have skin ulcers and diseases, which affects the important fishing industry based around the north and east of Scotland. Now the eight countries around the North Sea meet regularly and have introduced measures to reduce pollution and clean up the sea.

Sewage pollution on Blackpool beach is a serious threat to the seaside resort's tourist industry.

'Three-quarters of the sewage from Britain's coastal towns and cities is discharged raw, without even minimal treatment. Bathing in water contaminated by sewage causes gastro-intestinal infections, particularly in children under five, and may lead to ear, eye and skin diseases.' **– Hinrichsen, D. & Lean, G., Atlas of the Environment, (WWF/Helicon, 1992)**

The Empire and industrialization

During the eighteenth century, Britain gained an empire by colonizing large parts of North America, Africa and Asia. By the nineteenth century, England was bringing back much wealth from these colonies. The most profitable trade of all was the triangular trade between Britain, Africa and the West Indies. Ships from England took cloth, guns, rum and metal goods to West Africa. Here, they exchanged these goods for slaves. The ships then carried the slaves from Africa to the West Indies or America. Conditions on these slave ships were so bad that often half the slaves died on the voyage, but the traders still made a profit. In the West Indies the ships picked up sugar, cotton and tobacco and carried these to Liverpool and Bristol. There, they sold them to be made into rum and cloth, which were then traded back to Africa for more slaves, completing the triangle. The trade in slaves and other goods from the colonies supplied the money to build the factories and machines of Britain's Industrial Revolution.

'India used to make cotton cloth, but when it became part of the British Empire, taxes on Indian cloth went up and up. So it was cheaper for India to send its raw cotton to Lancashire to be spun and woven and then to have it sent back. In this way the Lancashire men and women got jobs, the British cotton merchants got the profits and the Indian clothmakers went out of business.' – **J.S. Stuart, The Unequal Third, (Edward Arnold, 1991)**

An engraving showing cotton-spinning machinery inside Dean Mills, Lancashire, in the nineteenth century. The large machines invented in the nineteenth century needed new, purpose-built factories, which sprang up throughout northern Britain.

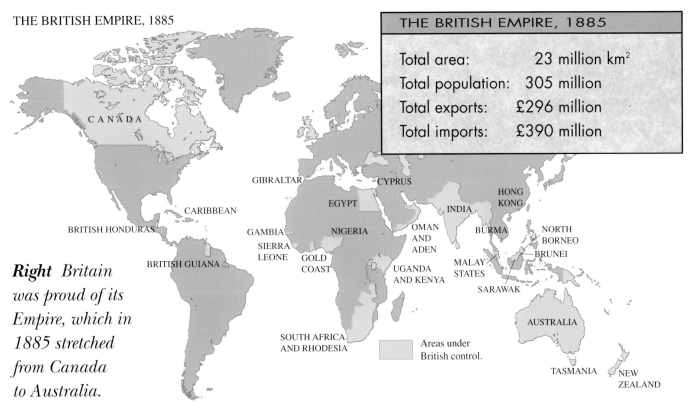

THE BRITISH EMPIRE, 1885	
Total area:	23 million km²
Total population:	305 million
Total exports:	£296 million
Total imports:	£390 million

Right Britain was proud of its Empire, which in 1885 stretched from Canada to Australia.

Areas under British control.

FIRST INDUSTRIAL NATION

In 1801, when Britain's first census was held, 10 million people lived in Britain. At that time most people still lived in the countryside and worked on farms. The Industrial Revolution, which began in the 1760s, was to transform the whole country. The invention of new machines to spin and weave cotton and wool, using water power and later steam, led to the growth of large factories in Lancashire and Yorkshire. Later, the use of coal to power the steam-engines and blast furnaces was the basis of the Industrial Revolution. New factories grew up on the coalfields of Central Scotland, northern England, South Wales and the Midlands. Cities like Swansea, Glasgow, Manchester and Leeds grew rapidly as people left the countryside to find better-paid jobs in the new factories there.

Below Victorian mills in Manchester, from the city's days as a centre of textile production.

Rhondda Valley, in Wales, 1900. Wales was the main coal-mining region in Britain during the nineteenth century. The rows of terraced houses in this picture were built for the coal miners of the valley.

By 1901 Britain had changed enormously. Most of the 37 million people lived in cities in the Midlands and in northern England. The country had by then developed heavy industries such as coal-mining, iron and steel manufacturing, engineering and shipbuilding, as well as textile and chemical production.

THE BRITISH CLASS SYSTEM

In the past, Britain had a very rigid class system in its society. The upper class were the rich and powerful people who made up the nobility. The middle class were business people and professionals, with moderate incomes, who usually worked in shops and offices. Their numbers increased during the nineteenth century and into the twentieth century with the growth of trade, industry and public administration. The lower, or working class, were the poor who did the manual work in homes, farms and factories. This system lasted throughout the nineteenth century and into the twentieth century, and the definition of class only started to become less distinct after the Second World War.

Britain had become a wealthy and powerful nation as a result of the Industrial Revolution. However, conditions changed at the end of the nineteenth century and in the early years of the twentieth century, as a result of a number of different influences. Other countries, such as Germany, Russia, the USA and France had their own industrial revolutions and became major manufacturing nations. They began to compete with Britain in overseas markets. Countries to which Britain had exported goods such as coal and cotton cloth began to develop their own sources of energy, and their own industries. So British exports declined. In addition, Britain did not invest enough in new methods and technologies to face the new competition. So between the end of the First World War in 1918, and the start of the Second World War in 1939, British industry declined.

After the end of the Second World War in 1945, as Britain set about rebuilding its shattered houses, roads and cities, the National Health Service was set up. This government-funded service provided free health care, which poor people had not been able to afford before, for everyone. The education system was also restructured in the late 1940s to increase opportunities for children from poorer families.

This strike, by workers in Southampton in 1932, was one of the early signs that Britain's industrial miracle could not be sustained. As British industry faced competition from abroad, wage disputes and strikes increased.

From the 1950s onwards Britain's industries faced further problems. Many former British colonies in Africa and Asia became independent and established their own industries, affecting both Britain's imports and exports. The USA and the Soviet Union had become world superpowers whose industries dwarfed those of Britain. Countries such as Germany and Japan recovered rapidly from the effects of the war and rebuilt their industries using the newest technologies. As a result, their products were cheaper and better quality than those from British factories. Later, in the 1970s and 1980s, newly industrialized countries (NICs) such as Taiwan, South Korea, Singapore and Hong Kong became major exporters of textiles, cars, ships and electrical goods. This further increased the competition faced by British goods in world markets.

As countries in America, Africa and Asia regained their independence, Britain's power, wealth and influence began to decline.

THE LOSS OF THE EMPIRE
Independence dates of former British colonies.

The result of all these changes for British industry was rapid decline during the 1970s and 1980s. All over Britain, factories, mills, mines and shipyards closed and unemployment rose. This decline hit the main industrial areas of South Wales, Central Scotland, the Midlands, Lancashire and north-east England especially hard. Derelict industrial estates and high rates of unemployment created many urban and social problems. However by the 1990s, the worst of the decline was over as Britain began to concentrate on new hi-tech and service industries (see page 30).

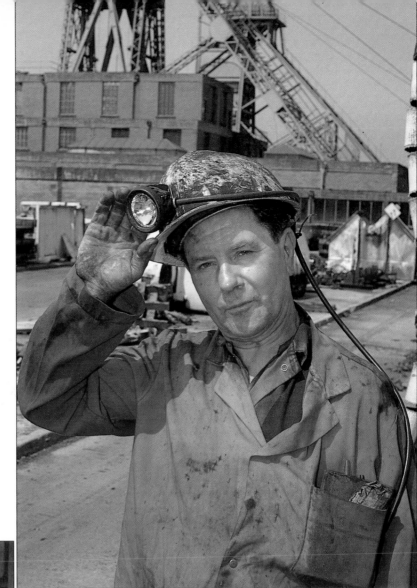

Above *Coal miners were one group of workers who suffered badly from the unemployment of the 1970s and 1980s.*

Left *A dole queue in 1976. Rising unemployment meant that more and more workers had to rely on 'the dole' – state unemployment benefits.*

Farming

With so many people living in a relatively small area of land, British farming has become very efficient. Some areas have specialized in a particular type of farming best suited to the local climate, soils and markets. For example, fruit is grown in the Vale of Evesham, in the Midlands, with its mild winters and warm summers. In general, the western parts of Britain have more grassland, so the farms raise beef or dairy cattle. In the upland areas of Central and North Wales, the Lake District and north-west Scotland, farms raise sheep or cattle. By contrast, in eastern areas, farms tend to be larger and to concentrate on arable crops such as wheat, barley and oil-seed rape.

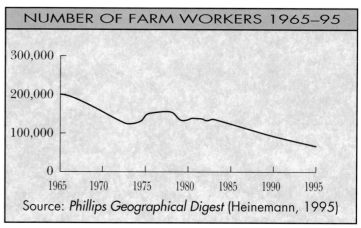

NUMBER OF FARM WORKERS 1965–95

300,000
200,000
100,000
0

1965   1970   1975   1980   1985   1990   1995

Source: *Phillips Geographical Digest* (Heinemann, 1995)

Farming is a large-scale industry in Britain. Only 2 per cent of the population are farmers (compared to 4 per cent in Germany, 7 per cent in France and 8 per cent in Japan), yet they supply all of Britain's wheat, barley, milk, beef, pork and poultry. Most British farms are highly mechanized, using tractors, combine harvesters and other machinery. They also use fertilizers to encourage high yields from their crops, as well as pesticides and herbicides to kill pests and weeds. Many animals, such as pigs, chickens and cattle, are reared indoors, where the farmer can control the temperature, light, air and amount of feed for each animal. This type of farming is called agribusiness.

The black-and-white Friesian breed of cattle has become the main milk producer of Britain. The breed originated in the Dutch Friesian islands and was introduced to Britain in the 1950s and 1960s to increase milk yields.

Modern British farming is large-scale, highly mechanized and employs relatively few people.

COMMON AGRICULTURE POLICY (CAP)

British farmers are subject to the Common Agricultural Policy (CAP) of the EU. The aim of the CAP is to give all farmers a fair standard of living while ensuring a reliable supply of food to the public at reasonable prices. The policy works by setting a guaranteed minimum price that farmers will receive for their produce, so they know they will be able to make a profit.

'Modern, intensive farming is not sustainable. It has been a purely post-war historic mistake driven by misguided government policies. It must end now.'
— Roger Martin, Director of Somerset Trust for Nature Conservation, 1992.

In the 1980s, the EU encouraged farmers to produce more maize, wheat, milk, beef and barley by setting high prices for these products. If farmers produced more than was needed by the EU, the surplus was stored. As a result, British farmers produced large surpluses, especially of wheat, milk and beef. By the late 1980s these surpluses, called 'mountains', had become embarrassingly large. So the EU decided to reduce the mountains by cutting the prices set for the products. At the same time, agreed maximum amounts of produce were set for farms to reduce production. These were called quotas. So in some ways, modern British farming had become too successful.

Some farmers have adapted to the EU policies by growing oil-seed rape, evening primrose, or lupins – crops for which CAP prices are still high. Other farms have diversified by turning themselves into 'pick-your-own' centres, while others have turned excess land into golf courses. Most recently, the EU has paid farmers to leave 15 per cent of their land uncultivated each year as part of a set-aside programme. This allows the land to recover from years of intensive farming, and also helps reduce surplus produce.

A plantation of fir trees on the Isle of Skye in Scotland.

FORESTRY

Only about 8.5 per cent of Britain (compared to 29 per cent of Germany and 44 per cent of Spain) is forested, and half of this was planted in the last forty years. Britain's natural forest cover has been cut

An Organic Farm in Wales

Reg and Barbara Price run Nevadd Fach organic farm in the Brecon Beacons National Park in Wales. In 1985 they became disillusioned with modern farming methods, especially with the use of so many chemicals in artificial fertilizers. So they decided to try and produce healthier food.

'I feel that a lot of farmers have forgotten how to farm and they rely too much on artificial methods.' – **Reg Price, organic farmer, 1994.**

Instead of traditional crops like barley, they now grow vegetables such as carrots and sprouts. The only fertilizer used on the farm is manure from the cattle and sheep.

Since Reg and Barbara cannot use chemicals to kill the weeds, keeping them under control is a major problem. They have to keep harrowing the ground to root out the weeds, but it is a slow process. Organic farming involves much more manual labour, but Reg and Barbara feel it is worth it.

down over hundreds of years, especially in the eighteenth and nineteenth centuries. As a result by 1914, less than 3 per cent of Britain was forested. During the First World War, Britain realized the danger of relying on imported timber since German submarines in the seas around British coasts threatened all imports. So in 1919, the Forestry Commission was set up to plant many more trees throughout the country. Since then large areas, mostly in the uplands of Wales, England and Scotland have been planted with fast-growing conifers such as pine, fir and spruce.

There have been objections to this planting policy, however, because the conifers change whole ecosystems, which affects plants, insects and the soil. The new forests are also vulnerable to fire and to attack by insect pests. So now the Forestry Commission tries to plant a range of different trees in one area, including deciduous trees such as beech and oak.

Harvesting potatoes by hand on an organic farm. Organic farming employs many more people at planting and harvest time than mechanized farming. However, for the rest of the year, these extra workers may have to find another job.

Becoming organic has meant big changes to the farm. In addition to their own back-breaking work, Reg and Barbara need extra labour to help with the harvest, which has to be done by hand. They also needed a new way of marketing their crops. This is done using a co-operative in the nearby town of Lampeter, which takes only the highest-quality produce and sells to high-street supermarkets.

'I really believe that you are what you eat. When you're living on a farm you see the chemicals-side of the industry and you realize the enormous amount of chemical input.'
– Barbara Price, organic farmer, 1994.

Power industries

Coal miners in an underground transporter on their way back from work at a coal face. In some deep mines, workers have to travel 2–3 km underground to reach the coal face.

Britain's Industrial Revolution was based on the coal industry, which at its peak in 1913 employed 1 million workers to produce 292 million tonnes of coal. Since then, the coal industry has suffered a dramatic decline because the best coal-seams have been exhausted, and oil and gas are cheaper and create less pollution.

COAL MINING

By 1995, the number of coal-mines in Britain was reduced to sixteen, employing only 11,000 miners, and the entire industry was sold by the government to private companies.

Most British coal is sold to electricity generating stations, who take most of the 30 million tonnes produced. However, the electricity companies find that British deep-mined coal is very expensive. British coal also has a high sulphur content compared to coal from other countries, which increases acid rain pollution. So cheap, low-sulphur coal is increasingly being imported from countries like Colombia, South Africa, the USA and China.

ACID RAIN IN BRITAIN

Acid rain is a type of pollution that occurs from the gases produced from coal-burning power stations. Sulphur dioxide and nitrogen oxide form acid when they mix with water in the atmosphere, which then falls as acid rain. This type of pollution is a big problem in northern and eastern Britain, because it is carried in the wind from power stations in the north-west and the Midlands. The pollution affects the growth of trees, kills fish in streams and lakes, and dissolves the stone-work on buildings. For example, St. Paul's Cathedral has lost over 2 cm in thickness of stone since it was built 300 years ago.

Power stations can reduce the amount of pollution they cause by putting filters in their chimneys to remove sulphur dioxide and nitrogen oxide, but this is expensive.

OIL AND NATURAL GAS

Oil and natural gas were discovered under the North Sea in the 1960s. Since then, both have become important sources of power in Britain, with oil supplying 45 per cent and gas supplying 18 per cent of the country's energy. In the 1990s, several new gas-burning power stations were built because the gas was cheap and, unlike coal, does not add to the acid rain problem. New oil and gasfields are still being found in the North Sea. Between four and twenty new fields will be developed every year for the next twenty years, and the petroleum companies have now started to search for oil and gas in the Atlantic, off the coasts of Scotland and Ireland.

Above Drilling rigs in the North Sea search for oil and gas deep under the ocean.

NUCLEAR POWER

Nuclear power only provides about 5 per cent of Britain's energy because, despite government support, it has proved to be a very expensive form of energy. Nuclear power stations are expensive to build and run, and are very expensive to dismantle at the end of their working lives. Most nuclear power stations have been built in remote coastal sites like Sizewell and Dungeness in England, and Dounreay in Scotland, but few new stations are planned.

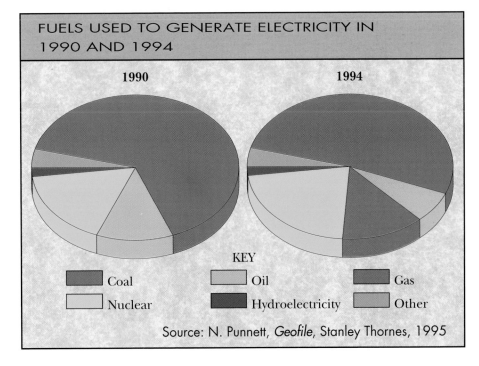

FUELS USED TO GENERATE ELECTRICITY IN 1990 AND 1994

1990   1994

KEY

- Coal
- Oil
- Gas
- Nuclear
- Hydroelectricity
- Other

Source: N. Punnett, *Geofile*, Stanley Thornes, 1995

23

Alternative and Renewable Energy

Concerns about the environmental damage caused by the traditional coal, oil and gas industries have prompted research into alternative sources of power in Britain. These are natural and renewable sources of power from running water, sunlight, wind and organic waste.

Hydroelectric power (HEP) is generated by running water. There are a few HEP schemes in the more remote parts of Wales and northern Scotland, but other regions do not have the rugged landscape necessary to generate HEP. Barrages built across estuaries such as the Severn and Mersey could use the rise and

A hydroelectric power station at Pitlochry, in Scotland. The fish ladder along the left-hand-side lets salmon through, to continue travelling along the river.

'More and more people, who still want their energy as cheaply as possible, now worry about the impact the energy industries are having on the environment.' – James Hann, Chairman Scottish Nuclear Ltd, 1994.

fall of tides to generate electricity, but they would be very expensive to build and would damage the local environments.

In the 1990s, new wind farms were set up in Wales, Cornwall and Scotland. Wind turbines do not create pollution like coal, oil and gas stations. Yet some people claim they are noisy and spoil the landscapes.

Another form of renewable energy is bio-gas – gas produced by the decay of organic waste in dumps. Britain dumps 20 million tonnes of organic waste each year into holes in the ground, and the bio-gas produced can be used to generate electricity or to supply methane gas to paper and brickmaking industries. At present, only 10 per cent of possible sites generate this bio-gas, so there is potential for rapid growth.

Right *A wind turbine used to generate electricity in the Orkney Islands, off the north coast of Scotland.*

Manufacturing industries

Between 1960 and 1990, Britain went through a period of industrial decline that has been called deindustrialization. This means that as the traditional manufacturing industries of textiles, steel, coal, shipbuilding and engineering declined, unemployment increased. In the industrial centres of South Wales, the Midlands, Yorkshire, Lancashire, north-east England and Central Scotland, thousands of mills, factories, shipyards and mines closed. This deindustrialization continued throughout the 1970s and 1980s, with 2.8 million jobs in manufacturing being lost between 1971 and 1989 alone. Deindustrialization continued into the 1990s with the added influence of economic recession. This meant that unemployment rose in areas like south-east England, which had not been so affected by the earlier factory closures.

'This time, after the blizzard of redundancy notices in recent years, they are mostly … young men, men in their twenties and thirties. There is nothing for them. Unemployment in parts of Motherwell is already touching 25 per cent.' – **Ian Bell, The Observer, *12 January 1992, on the closure of the Ravenscraig Steel Works in Motherwell, Scotland.***

Miners demonstrate outside Tilbury power station in 1984. Many workers went on strike in the 1980s, and picketed outside their workplace to stop others going to work.

Building work in London's Docklands in the mid-1980s. An area of 1.91 km² of the Docklands was made an Enterprise Zone from 1982–92, which meant incentives were offered to businesses to move there. The government investment of £1.7 billion had attracted £6 billion from private businesses by the beginning of 1996.

STIMULATING GROWTH

In an attempt to try and stimulate new industrial growth in those areas affected by deindustrialization, starting in 1981, the British Government set up a series of Enterprise Zones. These are certain regions which offer incentives to firms to attract them to move there. Incentives include freedom from certain taxes and fewer planning controls. Enterprise Zones have been successful in attracting new factories, which have created jobs in areas of high unemployment. These areas often have derelict factories and polluted land. So Urban Development Corporations have been established in places like Teeside, Leeds, Sheffield, Bristol and Cardiff to improve the environment and facilities of the area. Projects include new road building and the clearing of toxic waste. The corporations also attract private investment to build houses, factories, shops and offices.

   In Wales and Scotland there are Government Development Agencies which also aim to revive industry. These agencies offer grants and loans to businesses, and build new roads and factories. In the Rhondda Valley of Wales, the Welsh Development Agency has helped to reclaim and landscape twenty-one-year-old colliery tips whose sites are now being used for playing fields, modern houses and new factories.

NEW INDUSTRIAL GROWTH

In the last twenty-five years, micro-electronics has become one of the fastest growing sectors of British industry. This is a new phase of industrial growth which scientists have called re-industrialization. It involves the emergence of new, and often small firms, together with the growth of hi-tech industry and the use of advanced, computer-based technology. These hi-tech industries are concentrated in only a few parts of Britain: in a belt between Bristol and London, called the M4 corridor; around Cambridge; and in Central Scotland. The future of Britain as a manufacturing nation depends on its ability to develop and specialize in hi-tech industries such as aerospace, computers, electronics, telecommunications and biotechnology.

Modern industrial manufacture and design, as in this laboratory in Scotland, use the latest electronic and computer technology. New products can be designed and 'built' on a computer, which can then test the products before any actual construction takes place. For example, new cars are designed on computers, then tested for features such as aerodynamics or wind resistance.

Japanese Investment in Wales

Wales has been successful in attracting many Japanese firms to locate in the country. The Welsh Development Agency offers grants and loans to help new companies, and runs a vigorous publicity campaign in Japan pointing out the advantages of locating in Wales. Companies such as Matsushita Electric established their colour

The Panasonic factory was built in 1976 in Cardiff, and now employs over 2,100 workers producing televisions and microwaves. Government grants and loans were important factors in attracting Japanese firms to Wales.

television (National Panasonic) and stereo tuner (Technics) factories in Cardiff in 1978. Later, National Panasonic music centres began production on the same site. Overall there are thirty-seven Japanese companies in Wales, employing over 9,000 people.

'*The Japanese connection now dominates over 80 per cent of the specialist, hi-tech areas of Welsh industry and commerce. The Japanese have brought much needed industrial diversification to the area, with over 300 new firms in the Rhondda Valley alone.*' – **John Chaffey in A New View of Britain,** *(Hodder and Stoughton, 1994)*

Lloyds of London is a world-famous insurance company. The development of new, electronic technology means that fewer employees are now needed in Britain's banking, insurance and finance sectors.

CHANGING INDUSTRIES

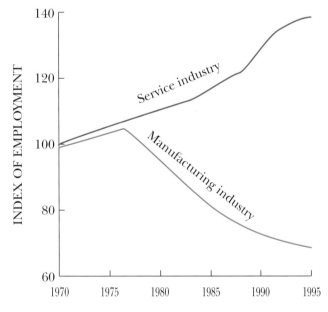

Source: *A New View of Britain* by John Chaffey (Hodder and Stoughton, 1994)

Since the 1950s, employment in Britain's service industries has increased at the same time as employment in manufacturing has decreased. By 1991, 70 per cent of the British labour force worked in service industries. Service industries include many different types of employment, such as banking and finance, transport and shops, together with health, education, and the tourist industry.

Service industries are heavily concentrated in London and south-east England, together with East Anglia and the Midlands. Central London has the largest concentration of service employment in Britain, with 5.5 per cent of the country's total labour force working with in a densely packed urban area of a few kilometres. London is one of the world's centres of finance, business and commerce. Growth in London's small area generates problems such as the high cost of office space and the difficulty of building a transport system that will be able to cope with a predicted 150,000 extra commuters in the next ten years. It is predicted that service industries will be the life blood of British industry in the 1990s and beyond.

30

Industry Growth in Bournemouth

Bournemouth, on Britain's south coast, has a long history as a holiday resort. However, in the 1980s and 1990s, it has attracted new financial services industries to make it one of the country's leading business centres. The traditional tourist industry provides permanent work for 12,000 people, and the 2 million tourists who visit Bournemouth each year spend over £250 million. In addition, Bournemouth now hosts a series of annual conferences which generate an extra £30 million.

However, it is the rapid growth of office-based industries that has really transformed Bournemouth. Five major companies have their national headquarters in the town and Chase Manhattan Bank has established its European headquarters on the outskirts of the city. Every day of the week, US $75 billion of business is transacted at the Chase Manhattan building. This has transformed the lives of local people, who used to have to commute to work in London, but who now have a short car journey to the new site.

'The growth of the Chase Manhattan bank and other service industries has been phenomenal. It's beyond the wildest dreams of the local council and Bournemouth is now looked upon as a model for other operations.'
– Martin Webster, Journalist, in the Bournemouth Echo, 1992.

The Bournemouth International Centre attracts businesses to hold conferences in Bournemouth, a traditional tourist resort.

Transport and trade

The private car is the most popular means of transport in Britain. Today there are more cars than ever on British roads – about 25 million in total. Britain has over 3,000 km of motorway and nearly 80,000 km of other main roads. Goods are transported mostly by trucks, rather than by rail or ship. However, the volume of cars and lorries has created traffic congestion and air pollution in and around urban areas. Some cities, such as Oxford, have tried to persuade motorists to leave their cars on the outskirts and travel in to the centre on public transport. These 'park-and-ride' schemes, together with bus lanes to speed up the movement of public transport, have only had limited success, however. Other cities, such as Manchester, Sheffield and Newcastle, have introduced electricity-powered light railways, or tram systems, which transport large numbers of people in and out of town and reduce pollution.

The numbers of cars on British roads mean that traffic jams like this one have become a familiar site on many motorways.

The British railway system has experienced problems of low government investment, ageing tracks, trains and carriages and increased competition from road transport. The rail industry was due to be privatized in 1996 – despite widespread public objections – in an effort, by the government, to increase private investment and modernization. New, high-speed electric and diesel trains are needed, together with changes such as computer signalling, for the thousands of commuters who depend on the British Rail services to travel to and from the centre of London and other major cities.

The Channel Tunnel gave a boost to the modernization of rail services in south-east England. Since its opening in 1994, the tunnel has reduced the London-to-Paris journey time from five to three hours.

Air transport in Britain is also important, especially for passengers between major cities like London, Glasgow, Birmingham and Edinburgh. Air freight is also increasing, mainly for perishable and valuable cargoes such as fresh fruit.

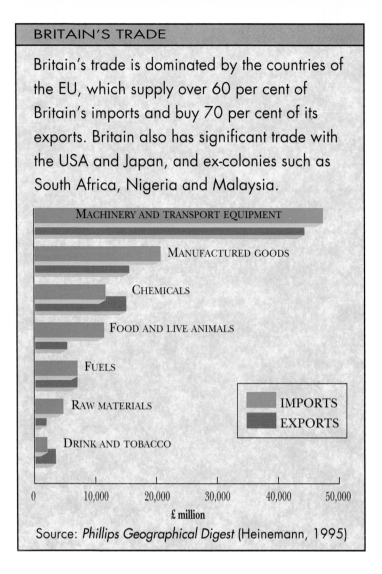

BRITAIN'S TRADE

Britain's trade is dominated by the countries of the EU, which supply over 60 per cent of Britain's imports and buy 70 per cent of its exports. Britain also has significant trade with the USA and Japan, and ex-colonies such as South Africa, Nigeria and Malaysia.

MACHINERY AND TRANSPORT EQUIPMENT

MANUFACTURED GOODS

CHEMICALS

FOOD AND LIVE ANIMALS

FUELS

RAW MATERIALS

IMPORTS
EXPORTS

DRINK AND TOBACCO

0   10,000   20,000   30,000   40,000   50,000

£ million

Source: *Phillips Geographical Digest* (Heinemann, 1995)

Cars board Le Shuttle *train for the 27-minute journey from Folkestone, on England's south coast, to Calais in France. The distance under the English Channel is 50 km. The first paying passengers went through the Channel Tunnel on 22 December 1994.*

Daily life

Children in the Listerhill area of Bradford, where there is a large Asian community. There are many different ethnic groups in Britain, including Jewish, Asian and Afro-Caribbean communities. Each group adds parts of their culture such as dress, food and religion to British society.

Britain today has a multicultural society, in which the traditional class divisions are gradually being worn away. British society is changing much faster in the 1990s than in the past. What a person has achieved is becoming more important than which school they went to, or which group in society they are from.

In the 1950s and 1960s, many people from India, the West Indies, Pakistan and Bangladesh were encouraged to move to Britain to live and work because of a labour shortage. Britain needed as many workers as it could get. Many of these immigrants moved to cities such as Bradford, Birmingham and London, where the jobs were located. Unfortunately, they had to live in the more run-down parts of these cities, and faced prejudice from the local communities. Despite some improvements in this situation, conditions are still poor for some 2.5 million Afro-Caribbean and Asian people living in British cities.

TOURIST ATTRACTIONS IN BRITAIN

Seaside resorts, theme parks and museums are popular attractions for many British people at weekends or on holiday. The most popular attraction with no entrance fee is Blackpool Pleasure Beach, which is visited by 6.5 million people each year, followed by the British Museum, in London, with 6.3 million visitors. The most popular attraction with an admission fee is Alton Towers Theme Park, (2.5 million visitors), followed by Madame Tussaud's wax-work in London (2.3 million visitors).

EDUCATION

Education is very important to everyone in Britain. All children have to go to school when they are five, although many also go to nursery school from the age of four. Children must attend school until they are sixteen. There are two systems of education. One is free and funded by the government, (state schools); the other is private (called public schools), where parents pay fees for their children's education. Children attend primary school from the ages of five to eleven, before going on to secondary school. Most secondary state schools are comprehensive (open to all), although a few select their pupils on the basis of an examination. At the age of sixteen, children in England and Wales take GCSE examinations, and some continue with their studies to take further Advanced Level examinations when they are eighteen. In Scotland there are no GCSE or Advanced Level examinations. Instead there is a system of examinations called Standard Grades and Highers.

Most children over eleven years old in Britain go to mixed comprehensive schools like this one. There is a fierce debate over the best way to raise the standard of education for children in these and other schools.

Some students continue their education at colleges of higher education or universities. At present, this tuition is paid for by the government. However, attempts are being made to introduce a system of student loans, where students pay for their tuition with money borrowed from a bank, paying it back over a number of years when they are working. The government is keen to try and encourage more students to go into higher education, but the cost of loans can be a problem for many whose parents cannot help them financially.

'Secondary-school examination results have sparked fears that the gap between the best and worst schools is widening. The figures show a slight improvement in schools achieving five or more GCSE passes but also an increase in the proportion of fifth formers who fail to pass any examination at all.'
– Geraldine Hackett, Times **Educational Supplement**, *1995.*

HEALTH CARE

Britain has a system of free health care called the National Health Service. Under this system, all people in employment pay a percentage of their income to the government, which uses the money to pay for a nationwide system of hospitals, clinics, dental surgeries and family doctors (as well as unemployment benefit).

In the 1980s and 1990s, the National Health Service was restructured because it was proving very expensive for the government and had created long lists of people waiting for treatment. Private hospitals and private health care schemes grew up at the same time, catering for people who could pay for treatment. Some National Health Service hospitals and family doctors became self-governing trusts, with control over their own budgets, in an attempt to reduce both waiting lists and the costs of health care.

Members of Parliament (MPs) inside the House of Commons. The members of the political party that forms the government sit on the benches on the left of the photograph, while the opposition parties sit to the right. The Speaker of the House (centre) sits between the parties and controls debates.

GOVERNMENT

Britain is a constitutional monarchy, which means that the king or queen is the head of state, but political power is controlled by the parliament. There are two Houses of Parliament. The House of Commons has 651 members who are elected by the public for a maximum of five years. The House of Lords is made up of peers. Some of these are hereditary peers, meaning that their title is handed down from parent to child; others are life peers, who have been made lords for their own lifetime but who cannot hand the title on to their children.

CRIME IN BRITAIN		
Offence	**1981**	**1992**
Theft/handling stolen goods	1,804,200	3,122,400
Burglary	816,100	1,468,500
Criminal damage	448,400	984,800
Violent assault	108,200	218,300
Fraud and forgery	128,100	196,300

Source: *Key data*, (HMSO, 1994/5)

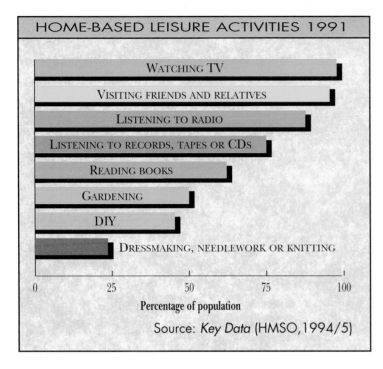

HOME-BASED LEISURE ACTIVITIES 1991

- Watching TV
- Visiting friends and relatives
- Listening to radio
- Listening to records, tapes or CDs
- Reading books
- Gardening
- DIY
- Dressmaking, needlework or knitting

0   25   50   75   100

Percentage of population

Source: *Key Data* (HMSO,1994/5)

The government is formed in the House of Commons by the political party that has the most Members of Parliament (MPs) elected by the public. The prime minister is the leader of this party, and she or he appoints a cabinet of ministers who supervise the day-to-day running of the country. The main British political parties are Labour, Conservative and Liberal Democrat. There are also Welsh and Scottish nationalist parties, who want to be separate from England.

SPORT AND LEISURE

Football, cricket, rugby, tennis and swimming are some of the most popular participant sports in Britain. As the number of working hours falls and leisure time increases, more sports facilities are needed.

Football is a popular sport both to watch and play in Britain.

Spectator sports are also very popular in Britain, either watching in person or on television. For example, an average of 393,000 people visit the Wimbledon two-week tennis championships every year; about 50,000 go to the Grand National horse race and 27,000 go to the Derby race.

British people are now travelling further in their leisure time to visit attractions such as country houses, theme parks and museums, as well as seaside resorts and national parks.

HOUSING

Most British people live in houses, although nearly 15 per cent live in flats. The oldest houses are in inner city areas close to city centres. Many houses and flats in these areas have been renovated and rebuilt over the last twenty years, but there are still many awaiting redevelopment. Large new estates of houses have been built in the suburbs and on the edges of towns and cities. Some of these housing estates have been built by the local government and are rented by the people who live in them. Many more housing estates were built privately and sold in the 1980s and 1990s. However, in the last five years, many people have been moving out of towns and cities to live in the countryside, encouraged by the urban problems of crime, traffic and air pollution. These people often face longer journeys to and from work to the nearest city, but they feel that they have a better quality of life by living in the countryside. As a result, rural villages have become centres of new house building, and the prices of existing rural houses have rocketed as the demand grows.

'The decay of our cities concerns me not just as a Londoner, but as a doctor because it generates a great deal of illness, depression and family disruption. It is made worse by the growing gap between rich and poor.' – David Widgery in **Some Cities, (OUS, 1991)**

Above *Many people are now moving out to villages like this one in Suffolk to escape the noise, dirt and crime of city life.*

Right *An elevated motorway cuts through a planned housing estate in the suburbs of Birmingham.*

New Age Travellers

New Age Travellers like these in Wiltshire are part of the search in Britain for a better quality of life. During the 1990s, people from all over Britain became very concerned about their quality of life. For some it has meant the change to a more mobile lifestyle which is freer from traditional problems such as the cost of housing and the search for jobs.

New Age travellers is the name given to groups of people who have opted for an alternative lifestyle. They do not live in one place, but move around the country with converted coaches and vans for homes. They prefer the freedoms of a life on the move in the open air. These communities work together to help and support each other. Often, New Age travellers will educate their own children, although some children do go to local schools. Unfortunately, the travellers have encountered opposition from local people in the areas in which they park. Complaints about noise and crime are common. However, the number of travellers has continued to grow. It is estimated that there are now 5,000 travellers in Britain.

'By definition the travellers do not want to stay put on a permanent site, so they are constantly on the move. Problems come when they park illegally in fields or on grass verges. Local people complain that the travellers bring noise, dirt and vandalism. We have to sort it out.'
*– **Roger Carter, Police Inspector, Staffordshire Police, 1995.***

SHOPPING

In the eighteenth century, Britain was called a nation of shopkeepers by the French general, Napoleon. But there are now much fewer shopkeepers than just twenty years ago. The reason for this decrease is the growth of superstores and hypermarkets which have sprung up all over Britain. Some of these developments, such as the Merry Hill Shopping Centre in the West Midlands and the Meadowhall Centre in Sheffield, have been built on the sites of old factories that have been demolished. Other new developments have grown up on the edges of towns where there was more empty space. The edge-of-town locations are also useful because there is space to build large car parks beside the stores and there are usually motorways or dual carriageways nearby, making them easy to reach by car.

'Shoppers are increasingly forsaking high streets and traditional town centres for vast, out-of-town shopping centres, built on sites that are legacies of Britain's industrial past. These shoppers decant [get out] in enormous parking lots and head indoors where the atmosphere is warm, bright, safe and synthetic, complete with security guards and splashing fountains.'
– David Stathers in **The Independent,** *1991.*

Traditional high streets like Eastgate Street, in Chester, have been modernized to make them more attractive to shoppers. The street has been pedestrianized to reduce traffic fumes and accidents, and to create more space for shoppers.

The rapid growth of these one-stop shopping developments, which offer goods from a number of traditional high street stores under one roof, has had a severe effect on the city-centre high streets. Many city-centre shops have been forced to close because they have lost so much business. They have the added disadvantage of traffic congestion and high parking charges which discourage shoppers. Now, however, city-centres are starting to fight back by cutting parking charges, and improving public transport, to win back the customers from the out-of-town superstores.

This shopping centre, near the M25 motorway in Essex, is easy to get to and has a large, free car park.

The Merry Hill Shopping Centre

Building started on the Merry Hill shopping centre, on the outskirts of Birmingham, in 1982, on the site of a steelworks that closed the same year. The site was cleared, levelled and made a government Enterprise Zone to attract new firms to the area. The first phase of development involved the construction of a large indoor shopping centre, together with retail developments that needed lots of space, such as DIY, carpet sales and fast-food restaurants. Later, the indoor shopping centre was expanded as large retailers such as Boots, Debenhams and Marks & Spencer moved in. The centre provides free car parking for 3,000 cars, has over 400 stores and provides employment for over 2,000 people. However, the growth of Merry Hill has been at the expense of existing nearby high streets, especially that of Dudley, where over 40 per cent of shops are vacant and boarded up.

The future

Café Cyberia is a café in central London where customers can gain access to the Internet and be served refreshments. The growing use of computers to store and access a vast range of information on the Internet is affecting leisure time as well as the workplace.

Britain is now emerging from a series of rapid and fundamental changes which have affected the lives of the whole nation. The government stimulation of new industrial growth in depressed areas, along with the massive growth of service industries, especially in the financial, shopping and transport sectors means that British industry is now more efficient and competitive in world markets. In the future, hi-tech developments will allow even more people to work from home, and commuting may become a weekly, rather than a daily journey.

Farming, too, is entering a new era. Having reached the point where it can produce all the food needed on less land, the emphasis is now on finding the best ways to use surplus farmland. Some has already been planted as new forests, and other land will be used for leisure activities such as golf and horse-riding. As environmental concerns increase, in future it is likely that farmers will be paid more to manage their land in ways that preserve the natural environment best, protecting wildlife and natural vegetation.

As the massive growth of out-of-town shopping centres and business parks draws to a close, the redevelopment of

Working from Home in the Countryside

Lisa Davis works from home in the village of Warslow, near Leek, using a personal computer (PC) to process data for companies. By working this way she is also able to look after her baby daughter, Mary. Her friends in the village, Sarah and Mark, also work at home. They are an accountants and a book-keepers, who maintain spread-sheet data on a contract for local businesses. They often meet together in the evening in the local pub, where the chat is about software, electronic mail and networks as well as local village gossip. Lisa's partner, John, is the manager of the village Teleworking Business Centre, which is housed in converted farm buildings. Part of his job is to run training courses in information technology (IT) skills. The centre has computers, electronic mailing facilities, fax, photocopiers, desk-top publishing (DTP) and database access.

'It's great working from home. I get to spend lots more time with my daughter, Mary, and as soon as I finish work, I can put my feet up and have a cup of tea. Even better, I don't have to sit for hours on end in long traffic jams to and from work, and I save lots of money on petrol or rail fares.'
– Lisa Davis, data-processor, 1995.

More and more people in Britain today are like Lisa and John, living and working in villages and earning money working for clients in London, Frankfurt or New York.

The use of computers has allowed more people to work from home. This is especially valuable to parents.

Britain's cities seems set to continue. This includes the construction of new city-centre shopping and office complexes and the renovation of suburban tower blocks and housing estates. A third stage of redevelopment will be to revive traditional city centres by building new theatres, cinemas, restaurants and leisure complexes.

The number of cars on Britain's roads looks set to continue growing, creating more pressure to build new roads and adding to air pollution. However recent government regulations on new cars demand they limit the amount of carbon they emit, and the building of light railways in towns like Manchester has helped to attract some people back to public transport. Some cities like Cambridge seem set to ban cars from city centres altogether in the near future to create pedestrian-only areas.

There is growing concern about the preservation of the British countryside, threatened by the rapid growth of towns, new roads and motorways. People are worried that some of Britain's most beautiful areas may be spoilt as a result of these pressures. More people are now aware of the need to protect areas such as national parks or country parks from further development and in future, more areas may become national parks in order to protect their beauty.

Manchester's light railway gives a fast, efficient, clean and regular service across the city, compared to the slow crawl in polluting traffic on the city's clogged roads.

Change always tends to bring insecurity, and the speed of change in Britain in the 1980s and early 1990s created uncertainty about the nation's future. However the success of Britain's hi-tech and service industries, especially within the European Union, has laid the foundations for future expansion and national confidence. Re-industrialization has become a reality, cities are being rebuilt, pollution reduced, and steps taken to protect the countryside. For the first time in the recent past, Britain seems to have to come to terms with its new industries and the new futures these can provide.

Snowdonia National Park in Wales is protected as an area of outstanding natural beauty.

'Britain's future lies with its service industries, which now dominate employment … Britain has now redefined its role both within Europe and the world, and British people are now looking forward to rising living standards.'
– Peter Daniels, Professor of Geography, University of Birmingham, 1995.

45

Glossary

Agribusiness Modern, intensive farming, which uses chemicals and machines to increase production.

Arable crops Crops such as wheat, barley and oil-seed rape, which grow on land that has to be ploughed first.

Class system A system that divides up the population of a country according to income and social position.

Colonizing Taking control of another territory to make a colony.

Commuters People who have to travel some distance to and from work each day from one district to another.

Customs duties Charges made on exported or imported goods.

Ecosystems Communities of plants, animals and other organisms, and the environments in which they live and react to each other.

Empire A country's overseas territories, which it governs in order to make a profit.

Enterprise Zones Areas that receive special government help to create jobs and attract new industry.

Environmental Concerning the surroundings, including people, buildings, trees, rivers, coasts and lakes.

European Union (EU) Formerly called the European Community (EC) or European Economic Community (EEC), an association in which fifteen European states (Belgium, Denmark, France, Greece, Germany, Austria, Ireland, Italy, Luxemburg, the Netherlands, Spain, Sweden, Finland, Portugal and Britain) co-operate closely on economic, social and political matters.

Exports Goods sold from one country to another.

Grants Sums of money paid to people like students, farmers, or industrial developers, to help them with their work.

Heavy industries Industries such as iron, steel and chemical manufacturing, which involve large factories and heavy, bulky raw materials.

Hi-tech The most up-to-date equipment.

Immigrants People who move into a country to live.

Industrialization The change from most people working in agriculture to industry becoming the main employer of a nation.

Industrial Revolution The invention of machinery in the 1700s which meant products were made in factories rather than by hand at home.

National Park A large, mainly rural, area, whose natural scenery and wildlife are protected for public enjoyment.

Organic farm A type of farm that does not use artificial chemicals.

Peers People who hold a title of the British nobility, for example, duke, marquess, earl, viscount or baron.

Pollution The harmful effect on the environment caused by human activity, for example dirt and waste.

Privatized Made a profit-making business.

Quotas Set amounts of goods allowed to be produced, for example the amount of wheat that one farm can produce for sale.

Renewable energy Energy produced by a source that will not run out.

Toxic Poisonous.

Further information

Commission of the European Communities, 8 Storey's Gate, London SW1P 3AT.

Friends of the Earth, 26–28 Underwood Street, London N1 7JQ

UK Central Statistical Office, HMSO Publications Centre, PO Box 276, London SW8 5DT.

Books to read

Focus on Britain and the British by A. Ganeri (Watts, 1993)

Passport to Great Britain by A. Langley (Watts, 1995)

People in the Countryside by T. Champion and C. Watkins (Paul Chapman, 1991)

Rural Land Resources by Martin Duddin (Hodder and Stoughton, 1994)

The European Union by Chris Durbin (Watts, 1996)

The United Kingdom by David Flint (Simon and Schuster Young Books, 1992)

Teachers' and Study Guides

Geographical Eye Over Britain (age 11–14) (Channel 4 Schools, 1996)

United Kingdom and Kenya (age 11–14) (Channel 4 Schools, 1995)

Videos

The following videos are all documentaries for schools:

Changing Wales (age 11–14) (Channel 4 Schools, 1995)

Landmarks: Portrait of Britain (age 9–12) (BBC, 1995)

Over the Border (age 11–14) (Channel 4 Schools, 1996)

UK, Kenya and Physical Geography (age 11–14) (Channel 4 Schools, 1995)

ZigZag: UK Geography (age 8–10) (BBC, 1995)

PICTURE ACKNOWLEDGEMENTS

The publishers would like to thank the following for allowing their photographs to be reproduced in this book: Camera Press 33; Cephas 25; Eye Ubiquitous 7, 10, 24, 40; House of Commons Public Information Office Photographic Collection 36; Hulton Deutsch 17; Impact 13, 21, 26, 27, 29, 34, 39, 41, 42, 43; James Davis Photographic 31; Manchester City Council 44; Mary Evans Picture Library 12, 15; Scotland in Focus 6, 20, 28; Tony Stone Worldwide *Cover*, Title page, Contents page, 4, 5, 8, 11, 18, 19, 22, 23, 30, 32, 35, 37, 38, 45; Wayland Picture Library 14, 17.

Index

Numbers in **bold** refer to photographs.